D0983318

To _Sue_

Thank you for your
best & all your company
& love.

May God Grant

You His Peace

Love, Nalini

31/1/96

Billy Graham

PEACE
WITH GOD

WORD PUBLISHING
Dallas · London · Vancouver · Melbourne

Peace with God

Unless otherwise indicated, all Scripture quotations are from the King James Version of the Bible.

ISBN 0-8499-5075-9

34569 PLP 987654321

Printed in Hong Kong

CHAPTER ONE

The Great Quest

You started on the Great Quest the moment you were born. It was many years perhaps before you realized it, before it became apparent that you were constantly searching— searching for something you never had— searching for something that was more important than anything in life.

At the loneliest moments in your life you have looked at other men and women and wondered if they too were seeking—something they couldn't describe but knew they wanted and needed.

But you are not alone. All mankind is traveling with you, for all mankind is on this same quest. All humanity is seeking the answer to the confusion, the moral sickness, the spiritual emptiness that oppresses the world. All mankind is crying out for guidance, for comfort, for peace.

The way of peace have they not known," the apostle Paul says concerning the human race (Romans 3:17).

As we look around, we find
that there is little personal,
domestic, social, economic, or
political peace anywhere.
Why? Because we all have the
seeds of suspicion and violence,
of hatred and destruction
within us.

Peace can be experienced only when we have received divine pardon—when we have been reconciled to God and when we have harmony within, with our fellow man, and especially with God.

Through the blood of the cross, Christ has made peace with God for us and is Himself our peace. If by faith we accept Him, we are justified by God and can realize the inner serenity that can come to man through no other means.

When Christ enters our hearts, we are freed of that haunting sense of sin. Cleansed of all feeling of contamination and unfitness, we can lift up our heads secure in the knowledge that we can look with confidence into the face of our fellow men.

When a man's ways please the Lord he maketh even his enemies to be at peace with him (Proverbs 16:7). Even more important, we know that we can stand before God in the hour of our death with this same feeling of peace and security.

We devise elaborate schemes for security but have not found it. We grasp at every passing straw and even as we clutch, it disappears. In the restless sea of human passions, Christ stands steadfast and calm, ready to welcome all who will turn to Him and accept the blessing of safety and peace.

CHAPTER TWO

You Can Start Over

*E*xcept a man be born again, he cannot see the kingdom of God. John 3:3

If I could come and have a heart-to-heart chat with you in your living room, you perhaps would turn to me and confess, "I am perplexed, confused, and mixed up. I have transgressed God's laws. I have lived contrary to His commandments.

I thought I could get along without God's help. I have tried to make up my own rules and I've failed. The bitter lessons that I've learned have come through suffering and tragic experience. What wouldn't I give to be born again!"

If those words strike a familiar chord in your heart, if they echo the thoughts that have been moving through your mind, I want to tell you some glorious news. Jesus said you can be born anew!

You can have the fresh and better start for which you've prayed. You can lose your despised and sinful self and step forth a new person, a clean and peaceful being from whom sin has been washed away.

No matter how soiled your past, no matter how snarled your present, no matter how hopeless your future seems to be—there is a way out. There is a sure, safe, everlasting way out—but there is only one! You have only one choice to make. You have only one path to follow, other than the torturous, unrewarding path you've been treading.

You can go on being miserable, discontented, frightened, unhappy, and disgusted with yourself and your life; or you can decide right now that you want to be born again.

You can decide right now to wipe out your sinful past and make a new start, a fresh start, a right start. You can decide now to become the person that Jesus promised you could be.

CHAPTER THREE

Peace
with
God

*T*herefore being justified by faith, we have peace with God through our Lord Jesus Christ (Romans 5:1).

There is a peace that you can have immediately—peace with God.

The greatest warfare going on in the world today is between mankind and God. People may not realize that they're at war with God. But if they don't know Jesus Christ as Savior, and if they haven't surrendered to Him as Lord, God considers them to be at war with Him.

That chasm has been caused by sin.

The Bible says that all have "sinned and come short of the glory of God" (Romans 3:23). Unless you repent of your sins and receive Christ as your Savior, you are going to be lost.

*F*or God so loved the world, that he gave his only begotten Son, that whosoever [that "whosoever" is you] believeth in him should not perish, but have everlasting life (John 3:16).

It's not just head-belief. It's heart-belief too. It's total trust, total commitment. We bring everything to the cross where the Lord Jesus Christ died for our sins. He made peace with God by His death on the cross.

Are you at peace with God?
Or do the sins of your heart
separate you from God?

CHAPTER FOUR

The Way Back to God

The way back to God is not an intellectual way. You cannot *think* your way back to God because human thought-life will not coordinate with divine thought-life, for the carnal mind is at enmity with God.

You cannot *worship* your way back to God because man is a spiritual rebel from God's presence. You cannot *moralize* your way back to God because character is flawed with sin.

There is only one way back to God. Jesus said, "Except ye be converted, and become as little children, ye shall not enter into the kingdom of heaven" (Matthew 18:3). This is how to begin! This is where it starts! You must be converted!

There are many people who confuse conversion with the keeping of the law. It is impossible to be converted by the keeping of the law. The Bible says, "By the law is the knowledge of sin."

The law is a moral mirror, the gauge by which man can see how far he has fallen. It condemns but does not convert. It challenges but does not change. It points the finger but does not offer mercy. There is no life in the law. There is only death.

Examine your own motives before you decide that you are above reproach and living a life that absolves you from all need of conversion. Look into your own heart fearlessly and honestly before you say religious conversion is all right for some but you certainly don't stand to benefit from it.

Conversion can take many forms. Conversion may follow a great crisis in a person's life; or it could come after all former values have been swept away, when great disappointment has been experienced, when one has lost one's sense of power through material possessions, or lost the object of one's affections.

Or, conversion may take place at the very height of personal power or prosperity— when all things are going well and the bountiful mercies of God have been bestowed gener- ously upon you.

There are many conversions that are accomplished only after a long and difficult conflict with inner motives of the person. With others, conversion comes at the climactic moment of a long period of gradual conviction of their need and revelation of the plan of salvation.

Actually, biblical conversion involves three steps. Repentance is conversion viewed from its starting point, the turning from the former life. Faith indicates the objective point of conversion, the turning to God. The third step we may call the new birth, or regeneration, commonly called being "born again," which literally means being born into God's family

There is a vast difference between intellectual belief and the total conversion that saves the soul. To be sure, there must be a change in our thinking and intellectual acceptance of Christ.

There are thousands of people who have had some form of emotional experience that they refer to as conversion but who have never been truly converted to Christ. Christ demands a change in the way you live.

But even if you have an intellectual acceptance of Christ, and an emotional experience—that still is not enough. There must be the conversion of the will! There must be that determination to obey and follow Christ.

Conversion is so simple that the smallest child can be converted, but it is also so profound that theologians throughout history have pondered the depth of its meaning.

CHAPTER FIVE

The Peace of God

Everyone who knows the Lord Jesus Christ can go through any problem, and face death, and still have the peace of God in his heart.

When your spouse dies, or your children get sick, or you lose your job, you can have a peace that you don't understand. You may have tears at a graveside, but you can have an abiding peace, a quietness.

*B*e anxious for nothing; but in every thing by prayer and supplication with thanksgiving let your requests be made known to God. And the peace of God, which passeth all understanding, shall keep your hearts and minds through Christ Jesus –(Philippians 4:6–7).

Be anxious for nothing. How many times do you and I fret and turn, looking for a little peace? God's peace can be in our hearts—right now.

Colossians 3:15 says, "Let the peace of God rule in your hearts." Some of you believe that you know Jesus Christ as your Savior, but you haven't really made Him your Lord. You're missing the peace of God in your struggles and turmoils and trials and pressures of life.

Is the peace of God in your heart?

Whatever the circumstances, whatever the call, whatever the duty, whatever the price, whatever the sacrifice— His strength will be your strength in your hour of need.

Peace with God and the peace of God in a man's heart and the joy of fellowship with Christ have in themselves a beneficial effect upon the body and mind and will lead to the development and preservation of physical and mental power.

Thus, Christ promotes the best interest of the body and mind as well as of the spirit, in addition to inward peace, the development of spiritual life, the joy and fellowship with Christ, and the new strength that comes with being born again.

What a prospect! What a future! What a hope! What a life! I would not change places with the wealthiest and most influential person in the world. I would rather be a child of the King, a joint-heir with Christ, a member of the Royal Family of heaven!

I know where I've come from, I know why I'm here, I know where I'm going—and I have peace in my heart. His peace floods my heart and over-whelms my soul!

The storm was raging. The sea was beating against the rocks in huge, dashing waves. The lightning was flashing, the thunder was roaring, the wind was blowing; but the little bird was asleep in the crevice of the rock, its head serenely under its wing, sound asleep.

That is peace: to be able to rest serenely in the storm!

In Christ we are relaxed and at peace in the midst of the confusions, bewilderments, and perplexities of this life. The storm rages, but our hearts are at rest. We have found peace—at last!

CHAPTER SIX

Future

Peace

The Bible promises that there will be a time when the whole world is going to have peace.

But we're not going to have peace— permanent peace— until the Prince of Peace comes.

And He is coming. One of these days the sky is going to break open and the Lord Jesus Christ will come back. He will set up His reign upon this planet, and we're going to have peace and social justice. What a wonderful time that's going to be!

Isaiah predicted, "The government shall be upon his shoulder: and his name shall be called Wonderful, Counsellor, The mighty God, The everlasting Father, The Prince of Peace. Of the increase of his government and peace there shall be no end"–(Isaiah 9:6–7).

Think of it: no fighting, no war, no hatred, no violence. It will all be peace.

Do you know Christ? Are you sure He's in your heart?

Perhaps you have been thinking, "I want to be sure I have peace with God. I want to be sure that I'm ready for death. I want my sins forgiven. I want my guilt removed. I want to be with Christ when He comes and sets up His Kingdom."

It's all yours, and it's free. You don't have to work for it. "For by grace are ye saved through faith; and that not of yourselves: it is the gift of God: not of works" (Ephesians 2:8–9). Give your heart and life to Christ now. Do not put it off.

Make your peace with God today.

Mini books from Word

Angels Billy Graham

The Applause of Heaven Max Lucado

He Still Moves Stones Max Lucado

Laugh Again Charles Swindoll

On Raising Children
Mary Hollingsworth, compiler

Pack Up Your Gloomees Barbara Johnson

Peace with God Billy Graham

Silver Boxes Florence Littauer

Splashes of Joy in the Cesspools of Life
Barbara Johnson

Stick a Geranium in Your Hat and Be Happy
Barbara Johnson

Together Forever
Mary Hollingsworth, compiler

Unto the Hills Billy Graham